MALCOLM LITTLE

The Boy Who Grew Up to Become
Malcolm X

ILYASAH SHABAZZ

illustrated by A G FORD

atheneum
ATHENEUM BOOKS FOR YOUNG READERS
NEW YORK • LONDON • TORONTO • SYDNEY • NEW DELHI

atheneum

ATHENEUM BOOKS FOR YOUNG READERS
An imprint of Simon & Schuster Children's Publishing Division
1230 Avenue of the Americas, New York, New York 10020
Text copyright © 2013 by Ilyasah Shabazz
Illustrations copyright © 2013 by AG Ford
ATHENEUM BOOKS FOR YOUNG READERS is a registered trademark of
Simon & Schuster, Inc.
Atheneum logo is a trademark of Simon & Schuster, Inc.
For information about special discounts for bulk purchases,
please contact Simon & Schuster Special Sales at 1-866-506-1949
or business@simonandschuster.com.
The Simon & Schuster Speakers Bureau can bring authors to your
live event. For more information or to book an event, contact the
Simon & Schuster Speakers Bureau at 1-866-248-3049 or visit
our website at www.simonspeakers.com.
Book design by Ann Bobco
The text for this book is set in Adobe Caslon Pro.
The illustrations are rendered in oil paint.
Manufactured in China
0720 SCP

10 9 8
Library of Congress Cataloging-in-Publication Data
Shabazz, Ilyasah.
Malcolm Little: the boy who grew up to become Malcolm X / Ilyasah
Shabazz; illustrated by AG Ford. — 1st ed.
p. cm.
ISBN 978-1-4424-1216-3 (hardcover)
ISBN 978-1-4424-3304-5 (eBook)
1. X, Malcolm, 1925–1965—Childhood and youth—Juvenile literature.
2. Black Muslims—Biography—Juvenile literature. 3. African American
Muslims—Biography—Juvenile literature. I. Ford, AG, ill. II. Title.
BP223.Z8L57729 2013
320.54'6092—dc23
2011041514

To Earl and Louise
—Ilyasah Shabazz

To my mother and father,
Al and Gwen Ford
—AG Ford

Malcolm X was one of the most influential men in American history. But before he became Malcolm X, he was Malcolm Little. Malcolm was born on May 19, 1925, in the small Midwestern town of Omaha, Nebraska. He was born into a tight-knit family with parents who not only encouraged his natural curiosity as a boy, but also taught him lessons about discipline, fortitude, and self-determination.

Malcolm's father was Earl Little, but there was nothing little about him. Papa Earl was a strong, broad, and towering man. His smooth dark skin was as beautiful as the midnight sky. His voice resounded like gentle thunder whenever he spoke. His protection and guidance stretched up and around his family like the great live oak trees in his home state of Georgia.

Malcolm's mother was Louise Norton. Louise was born in the island country of Grenada, West Indies. It was a place known as the Spice Island, where the sweet smell of nutmeg and cocoa swirled together in the tropical air. Louise was a bright student who excelled at reading and math. She began asking questions at an early age about the mistreatment of people of color in her hometown. After Louise graduated from school, she left for Montreal, Canada, to join her uncle Edgerton, who was a co-founder of the Marcus Garvey movement. Followers of Garvey believed that all humans are created equal.

In Montreal, Louise met the giant gentleman named Earl Little. Both of them had traveled to Montreal, focused on joining the struggle for freedom and justice.

Earl and Louise were soon married. The happy couple moved to the rural Midwest, and soon became the parents of seven children: Wilfred, Hilda, Philbert, Malcolm, Reginald, Yvonne, and Wesley. Earl and Louise cherished their family and instilled in their children values of faith in God and self-love, of honesty and integrity, and of brotherhood and equality.

The Little children were happy, and romped endlessly around the Little home and land in Omaha, Nebraska. Malcolm was the middle child and, well . . . Malcolm was different. He was full of questions, a natural leader, and a fun-loving prankster—and along with his brothers and sisters, he was always up to something.

When Malcolm was four years old, something horrifying happened that he would never forget. One night, while the Little family was sound asleep and the percussive hiss-hum of the cricket's song whistled quietly in the darkness, the loud crackle of a blazing fire awakened them. Terror clutched Malcolm's heart as he realized the blaze was consuming their home.

Fortunately, Malcolm and his family escaped the raging inferno, and they watched in disbelief as their beloved home burned to the ground. They would later learn that the flames had been set by towns-people who disagreed with their family's beliefs about universal equality and justice. The fire was a sad sign of ignorance and intolerance.

But nothing would stop Earl and Louise Little from moving forward.

Despite the great loss of their house and all their belongings, they vowed to rebuild their lives, armed not with material possessions, but instead with optimism and faith. After all, Earl and Louise knew that possessions come and go, but faith, love, and perseverance would sustain them.

Earl purchased six acres of land in Lansing, Michigan, and set out to build a new home for his family. He would construct it with his own hands from the ground up. Earl built the house nail by nail and brick by brick, only buying a new piece of hardware when he had enough money to pay for it.

"Papa?" Malcolm asked. "How come we don't have windows in our house?"

Earl answered with total confidence, "Son, when we can afford the glass, our frames will be filled." He leaned over to look squarely into Malcolm's eyes. "All good things begin with a fundamental structure." From that moment on, whenever Malcolm felt the wind blow through those empty window frames, instead of wondering when the glass would come, he would think of his father's unstoppable optimism and faith.

Malcolm's father would preach about faith, self-reliance, and hard work to throngs of people gathered at local churches and assemblies. The grown-ups in the audiences listened intently, their eyes fixed on Earl, their ears on his words, and their souls on his message. With arms raised high and eyes piercing with sincerity, Earl Little stirred the deepest parts of their beings. Malcolm felt the electricity in the room as the dignity and self-respect of those in attendance would steadily rise. The meetings were charged with the group's collective desire to create their own opportunities and to lead better lives. Malcom's father reminded them that they were not merely the descendants of slaves, but that their African ancestors built some of the greatest civilizations ever recorded in history; and that they, too, could stand together to build a bright future for their children. These were lessons in hope and self-determination that Malcolm would grow to love. Malcolm sat with rapt attention as his father's uplifting messages proclaimed freedom, justice, and equality for all.

And just as Malcolm found inspiration from his father's speeches at church, he learned some unexpected lessons from his mother's garden at home. For Malcolm, the enchanted garden of Louise Norton Little was an entire world of its own, where even the most sluggish of ladybugs and the fastest scurrying ants were all equally treated like esteemed and welcomed guests at a family Sunday brunch. Here, savvy spiders busily crocheted their delicate webs along the foliage, allowing the strong Midwestern sunshine to cast pretty patterned shadows on the soft earth below. Geraniums dotted the field in the distance with peppy pops of pink and purple, as the crisp, blue sky and lush, green field connected somewhere far out in the horizon. In this sacred garden, beetles hustled about like harried businessmen on their way to important meetings, while snails lolled leisurely, as if they were on some kind of half-speed permanent vacation.

Here, Louise taught her children to love every living creature equally—large or small, pretty or ugly, busy or still, fast or slow, insect or plant. The garden was a testament to true and unconditional brotherhood from the earth on up to the sky, a daily lesson in acceptance and equality. Each living creature had a story, a purpose, a reason for being, and a beauty of its own. Through the majestic trees in the garden, Malcolm would also learn about the importance of roots: nature's anchors, the base of every living creature; and through the outspread wings of the chirping birds above, he began to see the power of possibility.

And so this special garden became a source of knowledge, a Little family sanctuary where lessons came each day like tiny droplets of sweet morning dew. Because Louise knew that the best way to teach a child was to give him or her a chance, she gave each of her children their very own little plot of land in the garden, where they would take care of their designated areas like proud and professional minifarmers. Malcolm and his siblings learned to plant, water, trim, till, and harvest the crops—

which, in turn, planted the seeds for hard work and their sense of self-
reliance. With their shovels and watering pitchers in hand, they nour-
ished their crops and cared for their herbs, fruits, and vegetables as they
would for any other living creature—with intention, dedication, and love.

Malcolm's favorite vegetables to grow were peas. He would spend
hours in the garden methodically combing through the rows of seed-
lings and sprouts, his little fingers digging ferociously into the warm

earth, making sure there were no earthworms squirming around down there. When his mother later served the fresh peas at the dinner table, Malcolm would flash a great big, gratified smile.

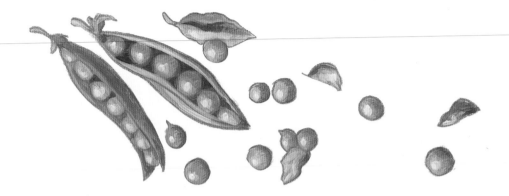

On one summer day, as Malcolm tended to his lot in the garden, out of nowhere a small flurry of color swept right through the air. As he stood up to wipe the August sweat from his forehead, Malcolm saw the colossal insect—it was every color of the rainbow—and it flew right by his cheek, as if to give him the tiniest kiss. Malcolm had never seen anything so pretty, its paper-thin wings forever winking at the world, its vibrant colors each one more beautiful than the next.

"Do you see that beautiful butterfly, Malcolm?" Louise asked her son as the breeze, insects, and flowers also seemed to stop in their tracks to listen to her speak. "Well, believe it or not, there was a time when that butterfly thought of itself as ugly, frightened, and all alone. It did not understand the value of its own little life. It had to learn about patience because it had no idea what the future would hold. It had to develop and mature and blossom. And now look at it—it's beautiful, proud, smart, and free."

Louise always found the time to instill lessons of good morals and values, even while she was ironing, washing, cooking, and fussing over all seven of her children. While folding fresh laundry, Louise would also unfold a newspaper from another country for her children to read, a window into the world and a way to connect with the rest of humanity—brothers and sisters all across the globe. Even though the children went to school, she knew that the best education they would receive would begin at home and that information was one of the greatest gifts she could give to them. She could bake biscuits while discussing philosophy, sweep the floor while reciting poetry, and teach math while pruning the garden. With one hand she would tend to the linens, and in other hand she would hold an open book, and Malcolm and his siblings would listen on as she enthusiastically taught them one of the alphabets of the five different languages that she spoke fluently. Malcolm especially loved the sounds of the letters in French and hearing the elegant intonation of this sumptuous language—words that to him always sounded like they were somehow dressed up. But most of all, these lessons in language taught young Malcolm that there was a whole wide world far beyond his noisy chickens and green peas.

DANAUS PLEXIPPUS

fig 56

You see, Louise Little knew the real truth about words. She knew that they were more than just a jumble of letters all lined up in perfect rows. She showed him the magic within words. She knew that each word was actually a powerful building block, a tiny gift of meaning that could bring ideas to life. She taught young Malcolm how to appreciate the dictionary and exposed him to the world of books. In each volume, ideas and inspiration mingled like the savory flavors in a Spice Island stew that Malcolm couldn't wait to taste. Louise knew that words had the power to move people, to make them laugh, cry, feel, and think. But most important, she knew that the more words you learned, the better you could communicate, and the more in life you could create. She firmly believed that knowledge acquired today would transform into wisdom tomorrow.

On sunny afternoons after school, when the air was still warm from the day and the chores were done, Malcolm loved to go fishing with his friend Big Boy. The two of them would stand over the stream like a pair of kings surveying their empire. They stood quietly, eagerly waiting for their fishing lines to move, for even just a hint of a ripple in the stillness of that glistening water.

Sometimes they would stand there for hours, watching the stream as if nothing else mattered. They would scratch their heads and exchange looks that said: What could we possibly be doing wrong? Malcolm and Big Boy knew that if they wanted results, they were going to have to come up with a clever way of catching the fish. What were they not thinking of? Malcolm would scratch his head, squinting through the sunshine, and mull it over with Big Boy, both of them trying to come up with a better way to attract the fish.

Then one day on the bridge, while their lines were still, Malcolm felt a rumble in his belly. The thought of the delicious supper that was waiting for him at home crept into his mind: *freshly baked biscuits, herb-roasted chicken, a medley of steamed vegetables from the garden, and a homemade apple pie with churned vanilla ice cream.* Malcolm imagined the aromas that would fill the Little house at dusk. And then suddenly it hit him. *They needed better bait!* Just like the aromas of dinner brought him and his siblings running to the table, Malcolm and Big Boy needed to lure the fish to come swimming to their lines. Their plastic earthworms obviously weren't cutting it.

The next day, just before Malcolm cast his fishing rod into the stream, he pulled a handful of bread crumbs from his pocket and hurled them into the water, where they landed like raindrops. Soon enough tiny bubbles appeared around the crumbs; and just like the Little children would come rushing to the dinner table each night, the fish swam around to see what treasures Malcolm and Big Boy had to offer. From that day on, the boys caught big beautiful fish, but more important, Malcolm learned that observation and effort could combine to create desired results.

But the innocent world of magical gardens and carefree fishing would be short-lived, and Malcolm's life would change forever.

The young boy, who until now had learned so much from his parents, lost his father, Earl, to the brute force of racism and the narrow-mindedness of Ku Klux Klan members and their brethren in the Black Legion. They disagreed with Earl and Louise's beliefs in equality, and

apparently they also disagreed with Earl's right to live in a free society. In fact, they did not seem to think that he had a right to live at all. And it quickly became clear that the hate and fury that was behind the fire that burned the Little house down many years ago, was now back again—only this time the hate was so strong, it took Earl Little away from his family forever.

Louise was left on her own to manage the household and the six acres of land, and fend for her children. She sewed, crocheted, and rented out garden space on her land. The oldest two children, Wilfred and Hilda, set out to help their mother with raising the younger siblings and keeping the Little family close and intact. It was the era of the Great Depression, and times got harder and harder. Soon local officials began to assert that Louise was no longer fit to care for her children, and they threatened to take away the family land. The proud, loving mother on whom the children depended was now being taken from them for reasons that no one dared to explain.

"When it rains it pours," Malcolm once heard his mother say. Now he understood exactly what she meant. When Louise was taken away, the Little children became wards of the State. All of the brothers and sisters were separated. Fortunately, Earl and Louise's good friends welcomed the children with open arms.

Without his parents' guidance, Malcolm became disobedient and required the structure of reform school. But due to his academic adeptness, he was eventually enrolled in Mason Junior High School.

When he arrived, he was the only student of color. Malcolm felt like a fish out of water. His brothers and sisters were gone. He missed the sound of his mother's voice. He longed for the passionate speeches his

father gave about the teachings of Marcus Garvey. He yearned to hear the gifted orator inspire people to care about history, justice, and equal rights for all mankind. As the only African-American student in his new school, Malcolm would have to blaze his own path toward discovering the remaining truths of his own identity.

Malcolm tried to cheer himself up. He would conjure up the sweet and satisfying crunch of his mother's oatmeal cookies after a long day at school

and the frenetic clucking of the chickens the Little family raised and sold, which always sounded like they were arguing. Now the memory of their squabbling provided music to his ears.

He thought of how funny Big Boy looked with his pant legs rolled up, sweat pouring down his cheeks like his own private rain shower.

Malcolm desperately missed the lively world of laughter and love that he had grown up in. He thought of his siblings—Wilfred, Hilda, Philbert, Reginald, Yvonne, Wesley, and his newest brother, Robert—the only other people in the world who must have felt exactly as he did. Malcolm wondered if they went to bed each night longing for the same thing that kept him awake—wanting to be together as a family again.

Sad, lonely, and confused, the beautiful colors of life he once knew flattened into an uninspiring shade of muted gray. The grief was stifling and nothing seemed to help—Malcolm was broken.

On one overcast morning Malcolm stood up from his desk chair and walked over to the open window, which was inviting a soft breeze into his room. He closed his eyes and took a deep breath, and when he opened his eyes again, he saw something that he would never forget. Hanging delicately from a small twig on a giant evergreen tree was a cocoon, something Louise had shown him one day in the garden. "You see that peculiar little thing, Malcolm? Well, it's actually a casing spun of silk, a protective covering for the creature that lives inside until it's mature enough to fly out into the world."

And just then, with one tiny wing at a time, a magnificent butterfly came half-fluttering, half-stumbling out. It was in flight for the very first time, set free from its home, alone, and finally face-to-face with the entire universe. When Malcolm saw the butterfly—that familiar symbol of freedom and transformation—he remembered who he was and where he came from; he remembered his own cocoon, the safe haven where lessons and values came like nourishment each day. With his eyes fixed, he followed the path of the butterfly flying away. At first it seemed uncertain, perhaps confused by its new life outside of the safe little shell—but in time it began to take flight, soaring through the world around it, bringing joy and color everywhere.

The soaring butterfly gently opened Malcolm's heart to feel joy again. Standing there on his own two feet, he felt his roots reaching down into the earth, gripping the soil and providing the strength he needed to awaken the dormant parts of his identity. He would use the sharpness of his mind to overcome the heaviness of his heart. He would replace sadness with smarts, and hardship with hard work at school. And just like the butterfly, Malcolm was ready to soar.

But his resolve would soon be tested. One morning the English teacher, Mr. Ostrowski, asked him what he wanted to be when he grew up. Malcolm, who was sitting straight up in his chair, proudly announced that he wanted to be a lawyer. His grades were certainly high enough to set him on this path. But his teacher did not believe that African Americans should have high expectations for themselves or aspire to excel. He did not believe that people like Malcolm should dream, hope, plan, or succeed. But Malcolm was now old enough to understand that Mr. Ostrowski was terribly wrong.

And just as nothing had ever stopped Earl, Malcolm learned how to rise up with that same bold determination that made his father a family hero. He had good ideas and good friends at school, and the can-do attitude to make something of that promising combination. Whenever Malcolm would tell a story or a joke, the kids would all gather around, their eyes fixed on the charismatic boy who was clearly different from them, but someone whom they adored and respected just the same. The little boy who had lost so much was now ready to face the world.

And then one day something extraordinary happened. Malcolm Little, the boy who was raised on the vision of freedom and justice, was elected class president by the students in his seventh-grade class! When they looked at Malcolm, they no longer saw a mournful child lost in the world; now they saw a smart, insightful, charming winner. They voted for a leader who believed in equality and who radiated optimism. Their open-mindedness symbolized hope for generations to come. you're actually joking

Malcolm may have lost his family, but he never lost the values for which the Little family stood, and for the rest of his life, whenever doubt, sadness, fear, or pain would come creeping into his thoughts— he would firmly hold on to one constant force that always gave true meaning to his family life: love.

Author's Note

I wrote this book for two reasons: to encourage young readers to access the transformational power within, as exemplified by the early childhood of my father, and to pay homage to my grandparents Earl and Louise Little. It was Malcolm's parents who provided the unconditional love and nurturance that would anchor his lifelong process of learning—forever aspiring to be better and to always give back to society along the way. As a daughter of Malcolm X, I have been privy to myriad stories of his youth, as told to me by members of my paternal family and by those who were closest to him. And since my mother, Dr. Betty Shabazz, devised ingenious ways to keep my father alive and present for the Shabazz family, the lessons and values that shaped Malcolm X as a man, a father, and a leader were indelibly impressed upon me from as young as I can remember.

Over the years, I have been invited to attend events, conferences, lectures, and workshops from people in all walks of life and from all over the world; and wherever I travel, the one common denominator I always encounter is that parents and guardians love their children. They want the best for them. They want their children to receive a quality education; to be respected as human beings; and to have equal access to opportunity—regardless of race, creed, or gender. My goal is to empower the little ones to feel good about who they are and to encourage them to live up to their highest potential—regardless of life's circumstance.

My father was born into a household filled with love from doting and attentive parents who were proud of their heritage. As my grandparents navigated the Jim Crow era of the 1920s and 1930s, they held key positions in Marcus Garvey's Universal Negro Improvement Association, a fact that my aunts, uncles, and father tremendously admired. My grandparents understood that a true knowledge of one's heritage was essential to a child's healthy identity formation. Instilling this value and emphasizing the importance of literacy, accountability, and leadership ideals in Malcolm and his seven siblings prepared them to live purpose-driven lives as members of the global family.

I have listened intently through the years as my aunts and uncles described their childhoods. In everyone's stories, Papa (Earl) loomed larger than life. Each one believed their father to be invincible, and they revered him as the family's strength and protection. It was Papa Earl who firmly established the family values of perseverance and accountability. He was a true role model, working long hard hours on the farm to provide for his family, and they all watched him labor late into the night as a Garveyite in the struggle for peace and freedom for all.

Louise worked equally hard to provide certainty and structure for the family. She insisted that her children build solid foundations in reasoning and analysis. Malcolm's mother found endless ways to stimulate their natural curiosities. She would use household chores and work in the family garden to teach basic education as well as pride in their heritage, and the critical lessons of tolerance and compassion.

I owe much gratitude and love to my relatives for helping me to clearly see my father—devoid of ideology, rhetoric, public perception, and controversy. I remember Uncle Wilfred, the eldest, always talking about Malcolm's kindheartedness, charm, and quick wit. Aunt Hilda relayed humorous stories about how her younger brother would cleverly coax the older ones to do his chores and how he would bounce up and down on Mother's bed, as if he were an Olympian. Uncles Wilfred and Wesley, as well as Aunts Hilda and Yvonne, remembered Malcolm as the fun-loving prankster for whom the world held endless adventures. They would all consistently talk about how smart Malcolm was. And Uncles Wesley and Robert, who were younger than Malcolm, would refer to their big brother as "brilliant!" They shared warm stories of the bonds between the siblings and of their close-knit family unit.

I have also had many opportunities to talk to my first cousins. They, too, have helped unravel the realities of our parents' youth. They speak proudly about our grandmother living with them after my father helped to get her out of the Kalamazoo Hospital. In fact, it is my cousin Steven (the son of my aunt Yvonne) who speaks most liberally about our grandmother's unique life path and how she left Grenada for Canada to be with her uncle, who was a co-founder of the Garvey movement, which is how she became recording secretary for the organization. My cousins Deborah and Sheryll (daughters of Aunt Yvonne and Uncle Robert, respectively) shared many photos and stories about their parents and our grandparents, as did my second-generation cousins LeAsah and Shahara Little-Brown, the grandchildren of Aunt Yvonne, who grew up in close proximity to Louise and lived with Aunt Yvonne for the remainder of her life, well into the 1980s. My five sisters,

Attallah, Qubilah, Gamilah, Malikah, Malaak, and I have reveled in the stories of our parents' youth to sustain us.

Given this vivid cache of memories and stories, the dialogue in this book reflects how I imagine conversations would have gone based on what my family knew of Malcolm's and Louise's personalities. I would like to thank my cousin Rodnell Collins, who conducted extensive research for his book, *Seventh Child: A Family Memoir of Malcolm X*, and for the countless personal discussions we have shared. I also gained insight and inspiration from *The Autobiography of Malcolm X*; *Malcolm X: Make It Plain*; and from the many letters written by my father, which are currently archived at the Schomburg Center for Research in Black Culture in the New York Public Library.

My father's collection of opulently colored butterflies encased in cherry wood and glass also proved to be an invaluable source of inspiration for writing this book. Each one of them was unique—beautiful, magnificent, and worthy of attention. Every time I remember their majesty, I am reminded that my father broke through the limitations of racism, injustice, and inequality to soar as an extraordinary human being. I say this not solely because he is my father, but because of his demonstrated love and compassion for all humanity. My father sacrificed individual freedom and personal gain to advance the cause of human rights. Malcolm X envisioned the world renewed by peace, and he denounced war and injustice as indefensible devastations of human and environmental resources. El-Hajj Malik El-Shabazz circled the globe in the final months of his life to advocate egalitarianism for all—regardless of religion, ethnicity, or gender. I share his youthful example of overcoming life's obstacles to ultimately achieve excellence and to give selfless service as a means to empower the achievement of each reader's fullest potential for the benefit of humanity. I believe the universal message of my father's life story will resonate with all children because it says *This is who I am: I am love.*